WITH A SKETCHBOOK

AT THE MATCH

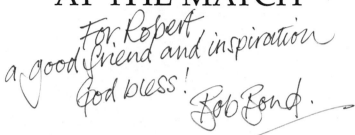

For Robert
a good friend and inspiration
God bless!
Bob Bond.

Some illustrated reminiscences

of following

Preston North End

in the 1950s

Published for Bob Bond by Verité CM Limited
8 St John's Parade, Alinora Crescent, Goring by Sea
West Sussex BN12 4HJ
United Kingdom
email: enquiries@veritecm.com
Web: www.veritecm.com

British Library Cataloguing Data
A catalogue record of this book is available from The British Library

Typesetting and production management by
Verité CM Ltd, Worthing, West Sussex UK +44 (0) 1903 241975

Printed in England

PROLOGUE

Back in the pre-rock and roll, make-do-and-mend early 1950s, when King George was still on the throne and ration books were yet with us, my mother and father took me to the Garrick Theatre in Southport to see Leslie Welsh the Memory Man. I sat open-mouthed at this man's mental gymnastics and the sporting facts and figures he had memorised. If there was such a word in those days, I was gobsmacked. A 10 year-old in the stalls had no way of knowing if he was correct on every point, or if indeed the questioners were genuine, or deliberate stooges. I wanted to believe that Mr Welsh was the real thing. Question after question he answered convincingly until someone asked "When did Southport win the Cup?"

That floored him…

There are still football anoraks like that, and they are to be admired and respected. And there are record books. If you want facts and figures, go there. This is not that kind of book. But if you want one man's rambling recollections of a golden age long gone, mixed with a few drawings, then this may be for you, even if you're not a Preston follower. It has been written largely from memory. In places I may have embellished fact and given it a lustre it doesn't deserve, and there will be inaccuracies.

The title is a little misleading. Only in later years did I take my sketchbook to the match. The drawings you see here, and the match cartoons, were done at a later date, and I suppose this book is simply an excuse to put them all together.

Happy reading!

CONTENTS

Dedicated to my late wife and lover, Margaret,
who for nigh on 50 years had to put up
with all my football daftness.

*" I have spent much of my life feeling intellectually superior to people who
follow sport. Bob Bond's writing merely justifies that prejudice."*

Steve Carroll, Artist, Writer, Thinker

CHAPTER 1

Paddy Waters ate my peardrop

Clutching my bag of Preston toffee bought on the market, I climbed the steps on the bus and ran to the front seat. You could see more from there. My Uncle Will followed me more slowly and sat a couple of seats behind.

"Now don't eat 'em all," he said. "Save some for thy mother…"

I knew my mother liked Preston toffee as much as I did. They were sticky and… nice. I was eight, and pretty grown up now. A big man came and sat next to me, and saw my bag of toffee.

"They look nice," he said, in a friendly kind of… Irish voice.

I held out my bag and he took one and thanked me. That was nearly sixty years ago and I hadn't been told about sweets and strangers, then. Anyway, it was me giving him one. He got up a couple of stops later, along Friargate.

"Bye, sonny!" he said, patting my head and disappearing down the steps.

"Do you know who that was?" asked Uncle Will.

"That was Paddy Waters!" he said, answering his own question.

Paddy Waters! I knew the name. Uncle Will had introduced me to Preston North End, and although I'd never yet been to see them play, I was familiar with the names. Ramscar, Gooch, McLaren, Waters… and, of course, Finney. My Uncle Will was an avid follower of North End. He went to every home game and on the Saturday evening he would come across the road and tell me all about it, and show me the programme of the match.

"How did Tom play?" I would ask.

"Magic!" said Uncle Will. Like all Preston followers in 1948, he worshipped Finney. At 26, he was approaching the height of his powers. The programmes were not as they are today… monochrome, just a few pages, teams in the middle laid out as they would appear on the field. The programmes cost 3d, not £3, but were just as romantic. When I got home after meeting Paddy Waters on the bus, I ran to the sideboard and pulled out a programme that Uncle Will had given me. Opening it at the right page I took it and showed my mam. Pointing excitedly at the name, I said "I sat next to him on the bus! Paddy Waters ate one of my pear drops!"

Mam was not impressed. "Cheeky beggar!" she said.

One Saturday evening, about a year before Paddy Waters ate my pear drop, Uncle Will had come in with a broad smile on his face. I didn't need to ask him if Preston had won. But I did.

CHAPTER 2

Fred and Judy lose the plot

"7-4!" he said, and as if I hadn't heard or believed, he said it again.

"SEVEN BLOODY FOUR!" That was Uncle Will's swearword, not mine. It was the only time I ever heard him swear, and that was in pleasure, not anger. I think that was the day I fell in love with Preston North End.

Others have written about a game that is part of Preston North End folklore. I wasn't there, but Uncle Will described it in such detail that I believed I was. Even now, at this distance, I know every see-saw swing of the game, and who scored every one of Preston's goals, and Derby County's too… But I still hadn't been.

My Deepdale debut took place soon after Paddy Waters ate my pear drop. I was still only eight years old, and Preston North End were sixty. My Uncle Will was a longsitting supporter. He'd seen them win the FA

Cup in 1938, two years before my first appearance in this world, and talked of it often. A terrible World War had coincided with my earliest years. I had lain in my pram shaking my rattle at Mr Hitler's Luftwaffe as it passed over our village on its way to bomb Liverpool.

It was good practice for all those days when I would stand on the terraces at Deepdale, a navy and white scarf around my neck and a football rattle in my hand. And this was the day...

"It's about time your Robert come wi me to a match," said Uncle Will to my mother.

"Oh, I don't know," she said. "He's nobbut a child yet."

My dad looked up from his Daily Express. He wasn't much interested in football, but he could see the pleading expression on my face.

"Aye, let him go. He'll come to no harm wi your Will. He's ready... "

Too right I was ready. I'd been waiting for this day. I'd been in love with Preston from a distance for some time. And my Uncle was now taking me

to a match. It might have been Ewood Park, or Bloomfield Road, or Haig Avenue even... but it was Deepdale, because they were his team. Those names I'd read in his programmes would come alive... Shankly, Gooch, Beattie, Langton... and Finney.

I'd heard more about Finney than any other player. I knew he must be somebody special. My mother gave me a bag of Holland's toffee as we left the house, and we walked to the railway station and caught the one o'clock train to Preston.

"Finney won't be playing today," Uncle Will announced mournfully as the train passed through Longton Bridge station. He hadn't had the heart to tell me until then.

"Why not?"

"Injured," he said.

It was a word I was to become all too familiar with. I'm not sure how much this news dampened my excitement, if at all. But the absence of Finney did affect Preston's followers considerably, and the attendance at Deepdale in later years.

Deepdale! We disembarked at Preston station and walked across the town to Deepdale Road. It's a long walk from Preston station to the ground, but that day my feet barely touched the floor. Preston North End's opponents would be Manchester United. I knew all about them. Why, had they not won the FA Cup earlier that year, beating Blackpool in an outstanding final? I'd heard Raymond Glendenning's radio commentary on that match. I'd wanted Blackpool to win, and Stanley Matthews, but United were too strong for them on the day. I could recite the Manchester United team as comfortably as any nursery rhyme… Crompton Carey Aston Anderson Chilton Cockburn Delaney Morris Rowley Pearson and Mitten…

In those days Preston's football ground was not so imposing as it is today, but it still seemed like a theatre of dreams to me… seeing the old wooden West Stand with its barrel roof as we approached, I already had a lump in my throat. Uncle Will bought his programme and we paid our money and clicked through the turnstiles. Then we climbed the stairs and came out again into the daylight. My first view of the pitch took my breath away… the green grass marked with clean white lines. Of course I knew what each line was called and what it was for… the goal line, the halfway line, the penalty area…

We sat down on the wooden benches, surrounded by other watchers.

"Paddy Waters isn't playing today, either," said Uncle Will. I wondered if he'd been poisoned by a pear drop.

"Nor Jimmy Gooch… "

Now that was serious, because North End's second string goalkeepers were either partially or totally inept. Jack Hindle had had a bad day against Manchester United earlier in the year in a cup tie at Maine Road. Willie Hall had had an even worse experience at the feet of the Blackpool forwards who had helped themselves to SEVEN at Deepdale. Poor Hall was so nervous at the end that he just lay down and let them roll past him. Again, I hadn't witnessed this debacle myself – I simply heard my Uncle Will relate the story, with a tear in his eye. Any loss to Blackpool was a tragedy, even then. 7-0 was cataclysmic. Malcolm Newlands was a better goalie than Hall or Hindle, but that's all that could be said in his favour. It's like saying that cardboard tastes better than cotton wool.

"Those people in the middle are season ticket holders," said my Uncle, pointing to the left. "They call that the Town End," he said, nodding to the right. "And over there is the Spion Kop." Already, with half an hour to kick-off, a large crowd was congregating on the Kop, with its crash barriers. The Brindle Band may have played before the start – I can't remember little details like that. It must have been the slowest half-hour I ever sat through, but eventually the players shot out of the tunnel underneath the quaint old Pavilion Stand opposite, like someone had let the cork out of a bottle of fizz.

The players looked stiff and awkward. The forwards aimed a few shots at goal, then jumped up and down to loosen their knees. Defenders casually passed a ball to each other. No doubt they'd done all their stretching and bending in the dressing room, cigarettes hanging from some of their lips. It was so not like today. Newlands looked nervous in the kickabout, fumbling shots and crosses. The portents weren't good. The captains shook hands, tossed for ends, which sometimes led to a complete turn around of the teams. The goalies, whether they knew each other or not, always shook hands as they passed on their way to the other end – a neat little tradition which always gave me a warm feeling inside. Then the game began with a rush.

My memory tells me that within a minute or so Preston were ahead, Bobby Beattie shooting past Jack Crompton at the Kop end. But that was as good as it got for North End as United methodically took them apart. Newlands confirmed all the supporters' fears with a trembling display. The visitors didn't need his help. Pearson, Morris and company scored six and then declared.

*Jimmy Delaney
and
Bill Shankly–
Scottish steel*

We went home sadly chastened. Uncle Will could always find some consolation, even in the worst of defeats. "I thought Shankly played well," he said, as the train chuffed out of Penwortham Cop Lane station. By rights, what I'd seen on my first visit to Deepdale should have turned me into a Manchester United fan for life. Their demolition job on Preston had been absolute. But I'd fallen for the men in white, despite the fact that they'd done little to earn my affections.

Preston were relegated to Division Two at the end of that season. Even a nine year-old boy can be devastated, as I recall. They say everyone can remember where they were when they learned of the death of some important person or other earth shattering events. I remember being taken to the pictures in Southport by my mam and dad on that fateful Saturday to see Irving Berlin's Easter Parade, but not really being able to concentrate on Fred and Judy and bonnets and things… the afternoon probably went something like this…

Fred: 'We would sail down the avenue, but we haven't got a yacht.'

Judy: 'We would ride down the avenue, but the horse we had was shot.' Bang!

Me: (thinks) 'I wonder how North End are getting on?'

Even on the last day my favourites could still avoid the drop if they won at Liverpool and other results went in their favour. We came out of the darkness of the picture house into the light and my dad, knowing my anxiety, bought an evening paper and I nervously turned to the stop-press. The news was bad.

"PRESTON WIN BUT GO DOWN," I read. I don't think I realised the full implications of relegation.

My Uncle Will was pessimistic when I saw him after Sunday School the next day.

"Finney won't stay now," he said. "He has his England future to think about."

PRESTON 1 UNITED 6

BEATTIE SCORED FOR PRESTON BEFORE MANY OF THE 37,000 SPECTATORS HAD SETTLED IN THEIR SEATS, OR ON THEIR FEET.

I THINK YOU MIGHT HAVE MISSED THE BEST BIT...

THE BRASS BAND PLAYED WELL, DID THEY?

THAT WAS AS GOOD AS IT GOT...

LONG BEFORE THE END MANCHESTER WERE TOYING WITH THE HOME DEFENCE. IT WAS LIKE A CHURCH WALKING DAY FOR THEM...

TO YOU, JOHNNY

TA CHARLIE!

AT 37, JIMMY DELANEY'S BEST DAYS ARE LONG OVER, BUT HE ENJOYED HIMSELF IMMENSELY, MAKING THREE OF THE GOALS. HE COULD PLAY MANY MORE SEASONS AGAINST SLACK DEFENDING LIKE THIS...

HOW MANY IS THAT? I'VE USED ALL MI' FINGERS ON ONE HAND...

INDEED, HIS DAD COULD HAVE KNOCKED IN SOME OF THE CHANCES HE SET UP.

IF IT'S THIS EASY TELL MATT TO SEND ME A SIGNING-ON FORM

MIND YOU, NEWLANDS IN NORTH END'S GOAL WASN'T AT HIS BEST.

DECLARE, WON'T YOU?

AND PRESTON ARE ON THE CREST OF A SLUMP RIGHT NOW

WITHOUT FINNEY, THEY LOOK JUST ABOUT GOOD ENOUGH TO BE RELEGATED.

TELL ME AGAIN HOW MUCH FUN WE'RE HAVING...

I'VE SPENT BETTER AFTERNOONS AT THE DENTIST...

CHAPTER 3

Short back and sides

Finney did stay, and though my loyalty was tested, so did I. The Flying Plumber realised that playing in the second tier would not affect his continued selection by England. Like other Preston followers I'd followed Finney's international career with involved interest, and particularly his contest for the number seven shirt with you-know-who. England solved their dilemma by playing Stanley Matthews at outside right and Finney on the left, to great effect.

I tuned in to Raymond Glendenning's crackling commentary from Turin in the Spring of 1948 and just about heard him describe one of England's greatest victories. When Finney scored twice in a few minutes to complete this triumph, I felt that inward glow. Our man, our Tom, was doing his stuff for his country, too. I have only fleeting recollections of matches during Preston North End's first season in the

Second Division, though I must have attended quite a few home games. I was not yet allowed to go alone, as I was not yet ten years old. My first sighting of Finney must have been in a match against Barnsley, early in the season. I don't recall him doing anything noteworthy, but just to see him run on the field was enough for this little lad. But I do remember Johnny Kelly, Barnsley's Scottish left winger, having a blinder and reducing Joe Walton to tears. Walton was North End's right back that day with Willie Cunningham on the left, although in time they switched. Kelly was folically challenged but could run like the wind, and was later immortalised by Michael Parkinson, Barnsley's biggest fan. Most visiting teams had at least one player of quality, and there was always a grudging admiration for them.

Johnny Kelly-reduced Joe Walton to tears...

If a non-Preston player did something clever there was polite applause and not, as happens today, a rude gesture towards him. Later in the season I watched Southampton's Charlie Wayman destroy Harry Mattinson with a classic display of the centre-forward art. More than anything it persuaded the management that he was just the man to solve Preston's goalscoring problems. Mattinson was promptly dropped, but to his credit learned from the experience.

I recall, too, the buzz of excitement when Preston paid out a record fee for the transfer of Eddie Quigley from Sheffield Wednesday. £26,500

Charlie Wayman
- a classic display
of the centre-
forward art.

seemed a colossal amount in those days – paid by a SECOND Division side! I saw his home debut, partnering Finney on the right, and to my recollection he was brilliant. But as the weeks went by the partnership didn't seem to work, and Quigley ended the campaign at inside-left. There were rumours that he and Tom didn't get on, but no one really believed that was the reason why Quigley failed to live up to expectations. He was a good player and later did great things for Blackburn Rovers.

It was towards the end of that season, which Preston finished comfortably mid-table, when I swear I saw Finney score a goal of rare quality against Hull City in a 4-2 win. In the eye of the memory I see a trail of defenders in Finney's wake, and at the end of his mazy dribble a shot placed carefully beyond the goalkeeper's reaching fingers. It was at the Kop end. Did it really happen like that, or does fancy run away with fact? In the immortal words of Max Boyce 'I know, 'cos I was there!' It was in that match, I give you my word, when Raich Carter, nearing the end of his illustrious career, provoked North End to anger with an action of extreme naughtiness. With Preston still arguing about the award of a free kick, Carter took the kick quickly and the ball was turned into an unguarded net by a colleague. The goal was allowed and spectators booed and catcalled the silver-haired Carter, but Finney answered in the most brilliant way.

...a trail of defenders in Finney's wake...

The Blackburn Rovers match on Easter Monday was played on an extremely muddy pitch, but Bobby Beattie mastered the conditions and scored two very sweet goals. I can still picture one of them now, with the Rovers' goalie beaten, face down in the mud. Or was that another goalie, in another match? Memory does play tricks on us sometimes...

But this is fact – the record books show that Beattie hit four goals against Blackburn that Easter weekend, and North End won both matches. Finney, too, must have enjoyed the day, as the Evening Post published a wonderful photograph of the Flying Plumber drawing three Rovers defenders to him, ball at his feet. It's possible to see water lying on the surface of the pitch, but Finney appears to have the ball under complete control and the three opponents under his spell. The Post called the picture 'The Magnet'. For many years a glossy copy of that photo hung up in the village Barber's Shop which I frequented.

'The Magnet'

Teddy Crook, the Barber, was a fervent Preston North End follower, and this picture of his favourite player held a prominent place on his wall. I must have stared at it scores of times whilst waiting to have my hair cut, short back and sides. Sometimes I went in to stare at it when I didn't need my hair cut. I marvelled at it. I knew the picture by heart. Even now, I can draw it without looking at it. Of all the hundreds of Finney pictures, this has to be my favourite one of all. God bless the photographer who took that picture. I would point to it, on the wall, and tell people proudly, 'When that was taken, I was there!' I can even see myself in the crowd, behind Finney. Or at least, I think I can…

'What makes you think
I'm not trying?'

CHAPTER 4

"You're football daft... "

1951 was an important year for me. I passed my eleven-plus, and in September went to Grammar School. As a reward my parents took me to see the Festival of Britain in London. It was the furthest from home my mother had ever been, and she had a nosebleed. They also promised me a season ticket at Preston North End. When this promise was made neither they nor I thought that in the August Preston would be back in the First Division. But they were...

They hadn't begun the 1950-51 season very well, but after Christmas embarked on a succession of victories that catapulted them to the top of Division Two. At 28 Tom Finney was at the very pinnacle of his career. Early in the campaign Wayman had been signed from Southampton, and he was the final piece of the jig-saw, and scored two goals against his former colleagues. Preston now had a team ready for the assault on promotion. There was no room in that team for Eddie Quigley. Instead, partnering Finney at inside right was local boy Ken Horton, who simply kept scoring goals. The fun really started with a 5-1 trouncing of Swansea Town. All five came in the first half, at the Kop end. Finney was irresistible, and as well as causing a visiting defender to score a most comical own goal, he rolled in one of his unique penalty-kicks. I'd watched him do the same earlier in the season against Grimsby Town and Sheffield United, always placing the ball to the right of the goalie with precision rather than power. I tried to do the same in a shool match a few days later, only to see my feeble kick saved easily.

Precision rather than power

Later in his career Finney varied his penalty taking methods, and he did miss from time to time. But when called upon to take a vital penalty against Russia in the 1958 World Cup Finals, Tom reverted to this early method and beat Lev Yashin's despairing dive. That was the incident where Yashin threw his cap at the referee.

5-1 was highly satisfactory, but in their next home game against Doncaster, Preston went one better. Then, as if that were not enough, they put SEVEN into the Barnsley net. I witnessed all of these one sided contests with great pleasure. I had an insatiable appetite for goals and had no sympathy for the poor goalkeeper. Angus Morrison was excellent down the left wing as Preston attacked from every direction.

I had no sympathy for the poor goalkeeper...

I was now a regular attender at home games. Nothing could keep me away. My grandad used to say to me "You're football DAFT!" and I guess I was.

Uncle Will didn't follow Preston on their travels, so I had to rely on Walter Pilkington's reports in the Post. By the middle of March it was clear that North End were going up. They were enjoying unbroken success with a run of 14 consecutive wins, seven at home and the same number away from Deepdale. The only blip was a defeat by Huddersfield Town in the Cup on a bone hard Deepdale pitch, Vic Metcalfe scoring one of the goals from a hotly disputed penalty... revenge for the 1938 Cup Final, perhaps? It was in this match that Harry Mattinson broke a leg, and he was replaced the following week at centre-half by Joe Marston. Mattinson, though an excellent stopper, never regained his place until the Australian went home four years later.

Apart from frost, Preston seemed to be able to play and win in any conditions… a carpet of snow at Maine Road, and a quagmire at Brentford, where Finney reputedly scored another goal of dazzling quality. Yet for all the wins and the goals and the records, the clearest memory is of Willie Cunningham sending a penalty-kick high into the crowd behind the West Ham goal. Although outplayed, the Hammers ended Preston's long unbeaten run in this match, and we had to wait until the next home match for them to clinch the title. Hull City were beaten by the only goal, a Finney special at the Town end. It was a season of unending delights, and I still think about it from time to time, and wish…

…another goal of dazzling quality…

CHAPTER 5

Matthews and Finney – on the same pitch!

Preston North End were back in the First Division, and as a reward for passing my eleven-plus I had a season ticket for a seat in the West Stand. It was a little book of tickets, and cost 42 shillings, I think. It wasn't known until we got to the ground which numbered ticket would have to be surrendered. The number was hung up on a board next to the turnstile. Seeing the long, winding queues waiting to pay to enter made me glad my parents had bought me that little book... Uncle Will had the seat next to me. I also started at Grammar School that Autumn. Ours was a rugby-playing school, and it was also a school which required us to attend on Saturday mornings. So to come home, grab a bite to eat and then rush to catch a train back to Preston in time for the kick-off was an exercise in gymnastic precision.

Preston's first home game back in the top flight was against Charlton Athletic and a crowd of more than 36,000 turned up that Wednesday evening. Finney was absent, but even without him North End peppered Sam Bartram in the visitors' goal. It took a blast from Willie Forbes, a half-back, to set them on their way to a 3-0 win. All was right with the world, and I had a spring in my step on the way home, and the next day...

A blast from Willie Forbes

Over 40,000 were in for the Blackpool match two weeks later. I think the gates were shut that evening, leaving many people outside. As season ticket holders, we were saved from that disappointment. Both Finney and Matthews played that evening. To see the two greatest players in the world on the same pitch at the same time – what a privilege! Within minutes of the kick-off Matthews sped past Will Scott and laid on a goal for Stan Mortensen. It was the only time in the match that Scott allowed him to do that. He was flawless, and the whole Preston team grew in stature as the evening progressed. Blackpool were beaten comfortably and, to rub salt into the wound, lost the return game at Bloomfield Road the following week. What else do I remember of that season? I recall Duggie Reid scoring a spectacular goal at the Kop end, one of two he got that day for Portsmouth. There was an excellent home win over

Matthews and Finney...on the same pitch at the same time!

Huddersfield, avenging the FA Cup defeat of the previous season and made all the more memorable by the curious fact of all five forwards getting on the scoresheet.

One mid-morning in February the whole school was called into the Assembly Hall and the Headmaster told us with suitable solemnity that King George VI had died in his sleep, and that we were to be given the rest of the day off. When she saw me coming down the road around midday my mother wondered why I was home so early.

"The King's dead," I said.

"Good Lord!" she spluttered. "God save the Queen... "

She didn't know. She hadn't had the wireless on that day.

A week or two later the Daily Express carried the headline:

'PRESTON SIGN LEWIS'. My heart skipped a beat... had North End really bought Reg Lewis from Arsenal? It turned out to be Derek Lewis, an unknown forward from Gillingham. If I was disappointed at first, I soon began to appreciate what a good player Lewis was. He was big, strong and brave, with a terrific shot, not unlike Duncan Edwards of a few years later. He wasn't as good as Dunc – who was? – but like Edwards his life was cruelly cut short. I really do believe that when Derek Lewis died Preston lost a player of real quality. Lewis's first game for Preston was against Manchester City, and coincided with an amazing display of goalkeeping by Bert Trautmann. He alone defied Preston that day as wave after wave of attacks bore down on him, and shots rained in on his goal. But thanks to the German ex-paratrooper, City escaped from Deepdale with a 1-1 draw when 6-1 would have been a fairer reflection of the play. Trautmann was made to suffer in subsequent visits to Preston. Angus Morrison scored North End's goal, one of twelve he got from the left wing that season. He was very direct and a good finisher, as befitted a man who had joined the club as a centre-forward. It may have been this season when he gave Alf Ramsey a torrid time in the match at Deepdale.

PRESTON 1 MAN CITY 1

TO SAVE YOU FROM FURTHER PUNISHMENT

GOOCH IN THE PRESTON GOAL WAS QUITE UNEMPLOYED.

THIS SCORELINE TELLS A BAREFACED LIE. THE MATCH WAS SO ONE SIDED THAT IF IT HAD BEEN A BOXING MATCH THE REFEREE WOULD HAVE STOPPED IT LONG BEFORE THE END...

HE HAD TO BE TOLD CITY HAD SCORED FROM THEIR ONE AND ONLY FORAY INTO THE PRESTON HALF.

BY COMPLETE CONTRAST BERT TRAUTMANN IN THE CITY GOAL PERFORMED WONDERS OF DEFIANCE AND AGILITY...

LIFE'S A JOLLY HOLIDAY WITH YOU, BERT...

LEWIS, MAKING HIS PRESTON DEBUT, MUST HAVE WONDERED IF HE HAD LANDED ON ANOTHER PLANET WHERE UP WAS DOWN AND BLACK WAS WHITE AND GOALIES WERE ANDROIDS.

FINALLY, FROM TWO YARDS, MORRISON DID GET ONE PAST THE IMMOVABLE BERT.

BUT IF PRESTON HAD PLAYED UNTIL MIDNIGHT, THEY WOULD NOT HAVE BEATEN BERT A SECOND TIME.

I EXPECT WHEN HE GOT HOME...

HOW WAS IT, BERT?

OH, JUST ANOTHER DAY AT THE OFFICE...

CHAPTER 6

"At number seven will be Anders... "

As well as being Coronation year, 1953 was an amazing year for sport. Stanley Matthews at last had his FA Cup winners' medal, Roger Bannister ran the mile in under four minutes, which we thought at the time was impossible, and England won back the Ashes at long last. And Preston North End SHOULD have won the First Division Championship...

What are my memories of that momentous year? It was a marvellous season for North End, and yet... so many opportunities were squandered to gain that extra point that would have earned them the title. In the very first match of the season Finney had a penalty-kick saved by Charlie Ashcroft of Liverpool. To balance this, Billy Liddell missed one in the same match, blazing yards over the Preston bar. Both these misses were at the Town end. I can see them now... So a point was dropped there, and the start of the season was quite ordinary for

North End, with only three wins from the first twelve matches. Newlands was still entrusted with the goalkeeping duties, Gooch having departed. But Newlands had two disastrous games in October, conceding ten goals. To lose at home to Manchester United was a regular occurrence in those years, but to be 5-0 down at half-time was embarrassing. Newlands, his confidence visibly dented, had to be replaced. George Thompson was bought from Scunthorpe United, and immediately the season was turned around. His first match ended in a 5-2 win at Portsmouth, and this should have been followed by a home win over Bolton. But with Preston leading 2-1 in the last minute the new goalkeeper grabbed Bobby Langton by the ankles, in the box. Langton dispatched the penalty, and North End lost another point. We didn't know at the time, thank heaven, that the title would be lost for want of one point.

He grabbed Langton by the ankles, in the box...

Another significant signing was that of Jimmy Baxter from Barnsley. He replaced the ageing Bobby Beattie. No one ever looked less like a footballer than Jimmy Baxter. Think of the ideal player – fast, broad-shouldered, strong... Baxter was none of these. With thin legs, small body and drooping shoulders, he strolled around the midfield. He was

Baxter...a comic figure.

Docherty...one of the club's all-time greats.

a comic figure, his face always wearing that hangdog look. My caricature of him isn't really caricature enough for Baxter. He couldn't wait to get off at half-time for a cigarette. Yet he could pass the ball as good as – nay, better than – Johnny Haynes. When the ball arrived at Baxter's feet, Finney or Wayman would set off running and know that the ball was going to come over their shoulder and land on the proverbial sixpence. I blessed the day that Jimmy Baxter signed for Preston North End. He was able to stroll around because in midfield he had Tommy Docherty and Willie Forbes to do all the heavy work.

The draw for the third round of the FA Cup that year was mouth-watering. Preston North End were paired with Wolverhampton

Wanderers... so one of these top First Division sides would be falling at the first hurdle. Fog swirled around Deepdale that January day, and when spectators arrived at the ground it was by no means certain that the cup-tie would proceed that day. The mist lifted in time to reveal a classic encounter. Finney and Billy Wright led out their respective teams, and a crowd of 32,000 revelled in the end to end action. Even the presence of the cool-headed Wright and the brilliant Bert Williams between the posts couldn't deny a rampant attack. The goals had been flowing for North End in those heady weeks leading up to this match – 18 in five games – and so it continued.

This was the team absolutely at the top of their game. I can't remember a period when the forwards were so irresistible. Charlie Wayman scored a hat-trick. It was his second at Deepdale in successive weeks, having scored three in the last 15 minutes against Middlesbrough to change a game that seemed to be heading for a goalless draw. His third against Wolves, just before the end, crashed into the net off the crossbar, thrilling, unstoppable, Williams face down in the Deepdale mud, beaten for a fifth time. In between Derek Lewis plunged headlong to score with a header which I can still see with my inside eye. And all the time there was Finney, teasing, tormenting, setting up chance after chance for Wayman and company, reducing the Wolves defence to raggedness and tears. The only solution was to bring him down, and Finney simply got up and potted the penalty out of the reach of Williams. Then he turned to receive the handshakes of his colleagues as he trotted back. There were none of the eccentric celebrations seen today when a player finds the net. Except on rare occasions, Finney seemed to show no emotions when he scored. The Pathe News cameras were at that match, so somewhere exists film evidence of what I and thousands of others saw with our own eyes. Or think we did. There were further epic battles with Wolves in the years to come, of which more later.

I was only eleven years old, and had just started at Grammar School, and all the talk amongst the boys was of Finney and Preston and of their chances of winning the Cup that year, which at the time seemed high… But it was not to be. Another home draw meant a visit from Spurs. There was no fog this time, but a howling wind which spoiled most of the attempts by both sides to play football. Blowing from the north, the wind greatly favoured the team kicking towards the Town End goal, which in the first half was Spurs. A man called Charlie Withers, who I'm sure was a kind man at home to his wife and children, scored twice. They were his ONLY goals in 200 appearances for Spurs! Why Preston, Charlie? The Londoners led 2-1 at the interval, with North End rarely able to get the ball out of their own half. Willie Cunningham's usual hefty clearances were caught by the wind and carried back almost to where they started. They did get upfield once, where Finney won a penalty and scored from it. Three times as he ran up to take it, the ball was blown off the penalty spot. Eventually, when Finney was able to strike it, Ditchburn dived to his right and caught it, only to fall behind the goal line.

Three times the ball was blown off the penalty spot…

It was the custom in those days to leave the ball on the centre spot while the players took their half-time break, and for some of them a cigarette. At the same time the Brindle Brass Band marched around the perimeter of the pitch, led by their familiar drum-major, twirling his baton and occasionally tossing it high into the air before catching it without breaking step. This half-time march was a feature of every home game, and the crowd watched and waited for him to drop the baton, but I cannot recollect this ever happening. It may have been on this day when the strong wind snatched the ball from its resting place and blew it towards the Town End goal. It would not have mattered had not the Band been coming to that very point of their circuit. The crowd were as hushed as when the ball came to Finney, wondering what he would do with it... it gathered pace, and I wasn't the only onlooker who had a vision of the entire Band being skittled, as by a bowling ball! At the critical moment a trombonist broke ranks and kicked away the speeding ball. The crowd cheered the best clearance of the day. Cup or League, Deepdale has known few such tense moments.

A howling wind spoiled most of the attempts to play football...

In the second half, with the wind now at their backs, the home side attacked in waves. There was an equaliser from Lewis, but no winner.

In those days in the event of a colour clash, and if it was a cup-tie, BOTH teams had to change into an alternative strip. Preston played in blue shirts that afternoon and Spurs wore stripes. North End lost the replay at White Hart Lane to a freak goal, and we had to wait another year for another assault on the FA Cup.

Under any other circumstances Harry Anders would have been a pretty good and useful footballer. A tricky dribbler, he could play on either wing to good effect. What he lacked in height he made up for in heart. The trouble with Harry Anders was that he was not Tom Finney. He would be the first to admit that he was nowhere near as good. He was apprentice to the best player in the world, and from time to time Anders was called upon to deputise for the Master.

"Here are the team changes from today's programme," the dread tidings would come over the loudspeaker, ten minutes before the kick-off. "For Preston, at number seven will be Anders and not Finney." The crowd groaned audibly. It was the least popular announcement ever made at Deepdale. I think, though I cannot swear to it, that some people got up and went home. I felt sorry for Anders, and sorry for the man who made the announcement. If spectators could have got to him, I think they might have lynched the messenger.

In January 1953 it was heard for the last time...

"At number seven will be Anders and not Finney."

Harry Anders played his last game for Preston against Newcastle, the Cup holders. He signed off with a stunning goal, from the narrowest of angles, that Finney himself would have been proud of. He then left Preston, unloved to the last, because he wasn't Finney, to join Manchester City. Anders later gave sterling service to Accrington Stanley in the Third Division North.

Anders signed off with a stunning goal...

The band would always play 'Margie' as Preston took the field before the start. For some reason unknown to me it was 'our tune'.

"Margie, I'm always thinking of you, Margie... "

The team would run out at this point, Finney at the head of course, one ball for every three or four players. Some of the crowd would sing the words, but it was not quite like the Kop at Liverpool...

"After all is said and done
There is really only one,
And Margie, Margie, that's you... "

Out of the FA Cup, Preston had only the League Championship to go for. But their successful run had given them a chance. In February Sheffield Wednesday visited Deepdale, with their scoring machine Derek Dooley. Dooley was a curiosity as well as a phenomenon. He had averaged more than a goal a game for Wednesday since his sensational entrance into the game. There hadn't been scoring on that scale since Dixie Dean plied his trade. Preston won the game, a Finney goal deciding it. But by that time Dooley had been stretchered off with a

41

broken leg, and the atmosphere was somewhat subdued. To this onlooker it didn't look much of a collision. Dooley chased a long ball towards the Town end goal and George Thompson just beat him to it. They collided, Dooley went down and didn't get up. At school, early the following week, the rumour went around that Dooley had had to have his leg off. The rumour turned out to be true. Gangrene had set in, and there had to be an amputation. Having seen it all happen I was badly affected by the Dooley incident, and even asked God what he thought he was playing at.

Derek Dooley - a curiosity as well as a goalscoring phenomenon.

I had a pact with the Almighty. If he would see to it that Preston won, I would be in Chapel the next day. As you can gather I was a good little Methodist and still am to this day. Preston North End were on my daily prayer list. When I'd finished praying about all the important things in the world, and family and school and the new Queen, then I invoked his blessing on every one of the Preston team, mentioning all of them by name, as well as a few reserves and even Harry Anders.

"Please let Tom be fit to play, and if you can't do that, let Anders have a good game."

But between us we just couldn't get North End home as Champions. In March they lost badly at home to Aston Villa. My memory tells me it was a rainy day, and Preston for some reason were not up for it. I have a picture in my mind's eye of a gentleman called Harry Parkes swaggering through the mud and through the match like a colossus.

Harry Parkes...
swaggered through
the mud like a
colossus.

Whether he scored or not I cannot say, but Villa, who finished only halfway up the table, severely dented North End's title aspirations that day. It still brings a sick feeling to my stomach when I think about it over fifty years on. Preston got back on the rails, and lost only one of their last eight matches, but the damage had been done. That one other defeat was at Charlton on a day when Finney was absent on international duty. That couldn't happen today. It was Preston or Arsenal for the Championship, and nearly 40,000 packed into Deepdale when the two met on the last Saturday in April. Preston did to Arsenal what they should have done to Villa, completely outplaying them and proving what we all suspected, that we were the better team. I can still see Finney's penalty going in at the Town end, and also Wayman's shot

Swindin went down painfully slowly...

beating George Swindin beneath the Kop. Swindin went down painfully slowly, like an ageing goalkeeper whose best days were long ago. But Arsenal were not wounded fatally. Their goal average was better, and although Preston won their last match, so did Arsenal a few nights later. Every North End follower at the time remembers the anti-climax, the switching on of the wireless, nervously, anxiously, only to learn that Arsenal had beaten Burnley and taken the title by such a narrow margin. I was twelve, and it was too much to bear. I hadn't yet found out about girls, but to be jilted at the altar couldn't possibly leave you with a feeling as empty as this. I went to bed but lay awake for a long time. Finally I convinced myself that it was only a postponement of the success Preston would surely have next season. After all, we had Finney...

CHAPTER 7

"Keep your hair on, Lambert!"

We were the train boys. Every afternoon my friends and I, carrying our heavy homework, walked from school back to the station to catch the train home. One Wednesday in November 1953 we made the same long trek, and asked the station-master if he knew how England had gone on. They'd been playing an international match that afternoon.

'6-3', he said. That figured. England could beat all foreign opposition at Wembley, so this scoreline was about what we had expected. Of course it turned out to be NOT what we expected at all. The Hungarians had given England a wake-up call with a scoreline which shook the whole football world. Finney didn't play for England that day. I doubt if even Finney at his best could have helped to make up the difference between mediocrity and brilliance. He was injured at the time, and Preston's season was turning into an up and down affair. Sheffield Wednesday were beaten 6-0, but this was partly explained by the fact that they played most of the game without Dave McIntosh their goalie, who was badly hurt. Full back Norman Curtis went in goal, and even saved a couple of penalties from Finney and Baxter, but couldn't prevent the avalanche. Preston also got six against Sunderland, but the performance I recall with most pleasure was at Liverpool. It was my second visit to Anfield, which for the opposition and their supporters was not so frightful a place as it would later become. On this occasion it was Preston all the way. Gordon Kaile scored his only goal for the club and Finney, after shooting yards wide from a penalty, got two wonderful goals in the second half. Each time, I seem to recall, he was put through by pin-point passes from Baxter.

Liverpool had a folically-challenged defender called Lambert, and the Preston fans continually invited him to "Keep your hair on, Lambert!" They thought it was so amusing. North End won 5-1, but it could easily have been eight or nine. But Finney couldn't stay fit, and played in only half of Preston's League matches. Dennis Hatsell made an encouraging debut, and scored six goals in his first six games.

Dennis Hatsell... six goals in his first six games.

47

Christmas was a bumper time for football in the 'fifties, especially at the turnstiles. Two games would be played, Christmas Day and Boxing Day, one at home and one away against the same team. Clubs could expect their largest attendances, and well over one million people watched a Football League match on each day. Preston usually played Burnley and there was always some needle in these encounters. North End kicked the Clarets a bit, and the Clarets kicked a few North End players in reply. So it was pretty even.

On this particular Boxing Day the goalies were brothers, George Thompson in the Preston goal and his brother Des between the sticks at the other end. When they shook hands at the cross-over, did it mean they got on with each other, or were they like most brothers? Burnley outplayed Preston at Deepdale but lost 1-2. In Finney's absence Eric Jones gave a passable imitation of the Master, and set up both goals.

Near the end the home goal had a charmed life, the ball striking posts and crossbar and defenders on the line but staying out. Brother George had clearly supped from some magic potion, rendering his goal impenetrable.

If Finney was top-billing, the one who continually pulled in and pleased the crowds, the rest of the cast were no mean players either. During those early 'fifties the half-back trio were magnificent. Tommy Docherty and Willie Forbes, both Scotsmen, arrived at Deepdale within a few weeks of each other. North End had tried a number of players at left-half, but none of them completely filled the position until Forbes came along, from Wolves, to solve the problem. He was the original bites-your-legs tackler. It seemed to me that few opposing forwards enjoyed an afternoon out with Willie Forbes. Normally great inside men like Logie, Hagan, Mannion, Broadis and the like kept as far away from him as they could. Others went down with mysterious injuries on the eve of the match. I cringed when Willie Forbes went into the tackle. But he was more than just a ball-winner. To see Forbes running with the ball, black hair flowing and shirt sleeves flapping, was one of the exciting sights inside Deepdale in those days. His passing was precise and at times he unleashed a fearsome shot. When he scored, once or twice a season, he was both surprised and delighted, running away,

...sleeves still flapping like a scarecrow

arms outstretched and sleeves still flapping like a scarecrow. If Forbes was an immediate fix, Docherty at first was a misfit when he arrived from Glasgow Celtic. Preston tried him on the wing, where he looked a square peg in a round hole. In that match when Charlie Wayman turned Harry Mattinson inside out, Docherty had a stinker at outside-left, and in the next few games, in the same role, if he didn't get any worse he didn't get any better. It was not the position God made him for. As soon as Preston erased their mistake and put him where he belonged, at right-half, the Doc became one of the club's all-time greats. His job description was quite simple really – to win the ball and give it to Finney. This he did wonderfully well week after week, season after season.

For four seasons, Joe Marston was quite simply the best centre-half in England. If he were English, he would have won a score of caps. Like Docherty he was played out of position to begin with, and the fans didn't like what they saw. I remember Joe in his first match looking like a fish out of water. But once he pulled on the number five jersey to

Joe Marston... coolness and calmness personified

deputise for the injured Mattinson, there was no doubting his class. Marston never missed a match for four years. He never scored a goal for Preston. I don't think he ever set foot out of his own half. But as a defender he was coolness and calmness personified, and utterly commanding. You felt somehow safe with Joe, like there was no need to worry. He was a rock, and was rewarded for his consistency when he was selected to play for the Football League XI. Joe Marston went back home to Oz in 1955. Before his last home game, I remember, the crowd sung 'Waltzing Matilda' with Marston standing on the penalty-spot looking embarrassed. I swear there were tears in lots of eyes that day, especially Joe's. Perhaps because it was so emotional, Preston lost the match 0-3 to Aston Villa, and if I remember rightly Tommy Thompson had a good game for Villa, and may have even scored. That summer he joined North End.

Half-time GALLERY

It's time for a break, and a look at some of the players from other clubs who lit up a golden decade of football...

DON HOWE HARD TACKLER, CLASSY DISTRIBUTOR...

ALF RAMSEY FELL OUT OF LOVE WITH ALL WINGERS.

BILL FOULKES, NEVER FLUSTERED, SAFE AND SECURE...

RONNIE MORAN NO WAY PAST HIM, FOR MAN OR BALL...

JIMMY ARMFIELD
GOOD ENOUGH TO SKIPPER ENGLAND...

WILLIE CUNNINGHAM

...MUCK OR NETTLES, ANY PORT IN A STORM.

A GALLERY OF FULL-BACKS

JOHN HEWIE
TALL BUT GRACEFUL SOUTH AFRICAN WHO PLAYED FOR SCOTLAND...

SCORING WINGERS...

PETER HARRIS— NEARLY 200 GOALS FOR POMPEY, AND TWO LEAGUE TITLES...

BOBBY MITCHELL THREE FA CUP WINNERS' MEDALS FOR NEWCASTLE.

PETER McPARLAND PERSISTENT IRISHMAN WHO ENDED PRESTON'S CUP DREAMS...

BILL PERRY, CUP FINAL HERO AND CHOSEN BY ENGLAND...

BILLY LIDDELL, CARRIED LIVERPOOL THROUGHOUT THE DECADE.

BRYAN DOUGLAS BUNDLE OF TRICKS FOR ROVERS, HE SCORED A BRILLIANT GOAL AT DEEPDALE...

EDDIE FIRMANI OF CHARLTON ATHLETIC — ONE OF OUR EARLIEST IMPORTS ...

INSIDE FORWARD PLAYLIST...

TOMMY HARMER

CHARMED DEEPDALE ONE EASTER MONDAY.

ROY VERNON, CONSISTENT SCORER FOR ROVERS AND FOR EVERTON ...

WALLY FIELDING— THE BALL STUCK TO HIM LIKE GLUE...

JOHNNY HAYNES

COULD LAND THE BALL ON A PROVERBIAL SIXPENCE...

ALLAN BROWN

MISSED THE CUP FINAL WITH A BROKEN LEG...

JIMMY McILROY

FULL OF IRISH CHARM AND CHEEK, A TITLE WINNER WITH BURNLEY.

WOR JACKIE MILBURN OF NEWCASTLE

OLD-FASHIONED CENTRE-FORWARDS

ROY BENTLEY, CLASSY, COMPLETE STRIKER WHO LED CHELSEA TO THE FIRST DIVISION TITLE...

DAVE HICKSON, BRAVE AND LION-HEARTED GOALSCORER...

STAN MORTENSEN, GOALS GALORE FOR BLACKPOOL AND ENGLAND.

TREVOR FORD... ...CENTRE HALVES KNEW THEY WERE IN A BATTLE.

DUGGIE REID— WOULD RUN THROUGH A BRICK WALL FOR THE CAUSE...

JACK ROWLEY— LIKE HIS BROTHER, JUST LOVED SCORING GOALS...

A GALLERY of GOALIES

BERT WILLIAMS, BRILLIANT, SPECTACULAR, FA CUP WINNER WITH WOLVES...

TED DITCHBURN, ACROBATIC, AGILE AS A CAT...

TED SAGAR— LONG-SERVING 'KEEPER AT GOODISON PARK...

FRANK SWIFT, LARGER THAN LIFE, FILLED THE GOAL FOR CITY AND ENGLAND.

SAM BARTRAM, IMMOVABLE LAST LINE OF DEFENCE DOWN AT THE VALLEY.

RONNIE SIMPSON, FA CUP WINNER IN THE 'FIFTIES, EUROPEAN CUP WINNER YEARS LATER.

HARRY GREGG, IDOL OF THE IRISH AND POPULAR CUSTODIAN AT OLD TRAFFORD...

RON BURGESS, WELSHMAN WHO PLAYED WITH A SMILE AND A SWAGGER...

GENTLEMAN JIMMY DICKINSON, A POMPEY FIXTURE, YEAR AFTER YEAR, DECADE AFTER DECADE.

ROY PAUL — WHEN HE TACKLED YOU, YOU KNEW YOU'D BEEN TACKLED

RONNIE CLAYTON, PRESTON-BORN, BUT EWOOD FAVOURITE AND ENGLAND REGULAR.

JOE HARVEY OF NEWCASTLE...

BILL NICHOLSON SPURS PLAYER AND MANAGER...

...LIKED LIFTING THE CUP, SO WENT BACK AND DID IT AGAIN,

...SCORED WITH HIS FIRST KICK FOR ENGLAND.

RAY BARLOW, TOUGH BAGGIE WHO SHOULD HAVE WON MORE THAN ONE ENGLAND CAP...

A FEW GOOD WING HALVES

CHAPTER 8

I go to London to see the Queen

The FA Cup was a wonderful adventure which sadly ended in disappointment. Preston were able to keep their best team fit and together for the whole of the journey to Wembley. I remember little of Rounds Three and Four. I was quite unwell over Christmas and the early part of the year, and rose from my sick bed to learn of a win at Derby, sparked by another exceptional goal by Finney. I do recall going to Lincoln on the train with Uncle Will, and being impressed by the Cathedral on the hill. Of the match itself I have little recall, save that it was very, very cold and I nearly had a relapse. I think it was in that game that George Thompson saved a penalty-kick.

"That was never a pelanty," Uncle Will would say.

Or, if it was a Preston player who was fouled,

"Pelanty, ref! That's a pelanty!"

He never could pronounce 'penalty' properly. He was kind of dislexic when it came to penalties.

...another exceptional goal by Finney.

Ipswich came to Preston for Round Five full of hope, but went away badly caned. They were in the Third Division South at the time, and had an Irish full-back called Jim Feeney who apparently had a cunning plan to stop Finney. The newspapers got hold of this, and broadcast it to the nation. One couldn't help feeling that if Mr Feeney did have a plan, he should have kept quiet about it. Mr Finney was clearly not daunted by the news, and on the day would not be stopped by anybody. Shooting into the Town end goal, Preston were four up by half-time and added

He should have kept quiet about it...

two more in the second half. At one point the visitors had only nine men on the pitch as two of their defenders had collided with each other in trying to stop the elusive Plumber, who was already out of sight. Both needed lengthy treatment. The half-time scoreboard had revealed the shocking news that Blackpool, the Cup holders, were losing to Port Vale, another Third Division side. Such tidings nowadays would raise a cheer, but then caused only a gasp of disbelief. Preston needed three games and a slice of good fortune to dispose of Leicester City in the next round. I remember bunking off school to see the first replay which was on a Wednesday afternoon. I can confess this now, as there can be no retribution. I don't think...

Charlie Wayman kept up his sequence of scoring in every round, and did the trick once more in the Semi-final at Maine Road against

McIntosh clawing
at thin air...

Sheffield Wednesday. I recall his header going in, from a Finney cross, with McIntosh clawing at thin air. Preston outplayed Wednesday, Jackie Sewell and all, but it was well into the second half before their superiority turned to goals. On the way home from Manchester we rejoiced in the knowledge that Preston would be playing Port Vale in the Final. I, like everyone else, had blinked at the half-time score from the other Semi-final, showing Vale to be leading West Brom. Rumour had it that they had held on to that lead to the final whistle. Only later that evening did I discover the truth. It would be North End versus West Brom, who had in fact managed to turn the game around. A week after destroying Sheffield Wednesday at Maine Road. Finney was doing the same thing to Scotland at Hampden Park. Sammy Cox was the unfortunate left-back.

Cox was the unfortunate full-back...

There was a long wait between the Semi-final in March and the Final in May. I know there were tickets to print and allocate, and all kinds of other preliminaries, but six weeks was too long. There was time for Preston North End to lose their form, find it again, and lose it once more before the big day. Contrarywise, the Baggies found their form, lost it, and found it again. Whilst Finney was on International duty, North End stuffed Portsmouth 4-0, belying all the cynics who labelled them a one-man team. As a season ticket holder I would not have dreamed of staying at home because Finney was absent. At Easter, once again without the plumber, Preston won 6-2 at Tottenham, when reserve striker Dennis Hatsell scored his famous hat-trick. Of course, this led to calls from some quarters for Hatsell to play at Wembley, but Preston naturally went in with the same team that had done the business thus far. Preston had not had a great season in the League, but it was no mean feat to score five goals at Anfield and six at White Hart Lane. All the talk at school and at youth club was of Wembley, and of North End's certain victory.

Enough has been written about the Final, and the reasons for Preston's defeat. Instead of repeating what has been said by Finney himself, and others, I've included a few drawings...

Wembley Stadium, then...

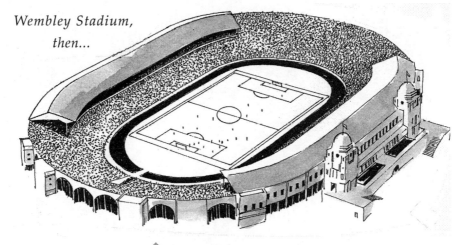

Saunders couldn't watch as Allen took his penalty.

Morrison... if only he'd been given more of the ball.

Not the Queen, but her mum...

Wayman looked offside, but he'd scored in every round...

It was painful for a 14 year-old boy to witness the Cup Final defeat and the manner of it. The journey home from London was interminable, and the thought that I would have to be back in school on Monday for English Literature and Latin compounded my misery.

CHAPTER 9

X-certificate viewing

North End scored 20 goals in their first five games of the new season. Wayman began well enough – a hat-trick in the opener against Manchester City – and all seemed right with the world. There was a surprising defeat at Everton, before a crowd of 76,000, the biggest I'd seen so far. I remember Cyril Lello winning the game just before the end with a shot that George Thompson should have saved. But a 7-1 win completed the double over Cardiff the following Tuesday, when North End were irresistible. All the forwards scored. Wayman had got six in six when the news broke that he had been sold to Middlesbrough. It took everyone by surprise. It seemed that the club expected Dennis Hatsell to fill Wayman's boots. Dennis did okay until Christmas and then fell away. Peter Higham scored a hat-trick on his first outing against Sheffield Wednesday, when Preston went 5-0 up by half-time. The next home game was with Wolves. North End and Wolves often served up thrillers during the 'fifties. For 75 minutes Wolves were magnificent and goals by Broadbent, Hancocks and Wilshaw put them almost out-of-sight at 3-0. In all honesty it could have been five or six.

Wolves were magnificent.
Hancocks, Wilshaw...

But then Preston began their fight back, playing towards the Town end. Finney won a penalty, and Baxter converted it. With minutes to go Bobby Foster forced in a second. In the very last minute young Higham shook off the attention of Billy Wright and lashed in a shot from the edge of the box, and Bert Williams had no chance. 3-3! We all went home buzzing after that one...

...and Broadbent all scored.

But Peter Higham gave Williams no chance...

I recall, too, that wonderful cup tie with Sunderland at Deepdale, which also ended 3-3, when both Finney and Len Shackleton scored terrific goals. Preston had just equalised at 2-2 when Shack picked up the ball, just beneath us in the West Stand, and quite deliberately lobbed George Thompson from about 30 yards. It was exquisite, and although it was scored against North End, the whole crowd applauded his impudence. Preston lost the replay at Roker Park. The same season Shackleton scored an equally cheeky goal for England against West Germany at Wembley. Why he didn't make more International appearances is one of soccer's great mysteries. I guess his face didn't fit.

Preston North End, and Finney, were such an attraction in the 'fifties that charabancs, or coaches, used to run to Deepdale on match days from outlying villages. One such ran from our locality. Because I was still a schoolboy I paid a shilling for this transport. Uncle Will, no doubt, was charged two shillings. Percy's coach was usually full, with sometimes boxes down the aisle if it was overbooked. There were five or six pick up points and then it would make the 15 mile journey into Preston, arriving at the ground 30 minutes before kick-off. Amongst the regular travellers were some real characters, and a lot of fun was had on the way to and from the match. Few people were able to resist voicing their views. Some players were universally loved – Finney, of course, and Docherty and Marston. Others divided opinion, and even in a successful team there were those who were cruelly criticised.

Arguments could become quite heated on the way home, especially if Preston hadn't won. Only once do I remember a blow being struck, and the perpetrator was banned from the coach thereafter. Someone would run a sweep which was won by the person who drew out of the hat the number of the player who scored the first goal of the match. The coach was almost entirely a male preserve. If occasionally a lady was present, the language was noticeably less colourful. Sammy Baird was a player about whom opinions differed. He was signed from Glasgow Rangers, coming with a big reputation. Clearly a good footballer, he scored a brilliant goal against Sunderland, but never quite made it in the English First Division. His only other goal was against Blackpool, on an ice rink. Games on such surfaces would not be played these days, but over 30,000 spectators saw the Seasiders well beaten with Bobby Foster having one of his best games for North End, scoring twice.

Shackleton... the whole crowd applauded his impudence.

By and large Preston had the beating of Blackpool in the Finney years, with twice as many wins as defeats. It all changed in the 'seventies of course, when Mickey Burns took delight in flogging his home-town team.

One foggy Boxing Day Burnley were due to be the visitors to Deepdale, but on arriving in the vicinity of Preston our coach-driver was informed that the match had been postponed. Rather than go home, it was decided by the majority that the bus would divert to another match on another ground. Someone produced a fixture book, and it told us that Everton, then in the Second Division, had a home game with Doncaster Rovers. It was a drab game, and ended 1-1. Dave Hickson scored for Everton and a man called Buckle nearly hit the corner-flag with a penalty. I don't know why I remember certain incidents like this. I guess we all do, inexplicably. It must have been my first visit to Goodison Park, in 1951 I think.

Speaking of violence, which I was a few sentences back, there was far less of it on the pitch than there is today. True, there were some very hard tackles and whole hearted shoulder charges that made spectators cringe. Preston had some players who could mix it if the occasion demanded it. But sending offs were few and far between. I do recall one Arsenal player getting his marching orders at Deepdale in the mid 'fifties, but he was one of only two or three to go in the whole decade. There were some who should have gone. Finney was kicked up and down by some full-backs who would not have survived more than ten minutes today. England full-back George Hardwick had a Clark Gable smile that disguised a tackling technique which would not have been

Hardwick... his Clark Gable smile disguised a terrifying tackling technique.

out of place in the Chain-saw Massacre. Our own Willie Cunningham was no wimp when it came to persuading his opponent to part with the ball. His sliding tackles were fearsome. They even made those of us sitting in the stand and those in the paddock momentarily close our eyes and wait for the yell. It was x-certificate stuff. Willie's feud with Billy Elliott of Burnley and Sunderland is part of Lancashire folklore.

The two Willies...

I recently watched the movie about the boy with the passion to dance, but all the time my mind kept going back to the REAL Billy Elliott. I have a memory snap-shot of the two Willies squaring up to each other while being restrained by their teammates, with the referee rushing to get between them, silly man. There would have been blood. And, if my memory serves me right, it was Christmas, the season of goodwill...

Waiting for the yell...

The half-time scoreboard was always a point of interest early in the second half. If spectators could take their eyes off the action on the field for a minute or two, it was possible to find out how Preston's First Division rivals had fared in the first half. The key to the scoreboard was in the programme, and two zeros under the letter A meant that Arsenal and West Brom had played a goalless first half. These scores were not displayed until after the second half had begun. The half-time interval was of only five minutes duration, not fifteen as it is today. These days there are many ways of keeping up with scores in other matches, but then we relied entirely on the half-time scoreboard.

The half-time scoreboard was always a point of interest

In the same way, if our team was playing away from home, we waited impatiently for 'Sports Report'. The BBC Light Programme always broadcast a commentary on the second half of one of the top matches, and sometimes it would be Preston. If not, there was the waiting and the wondering.

"It's five o'clock, and it's Sports Report!"...

and then would follow that familiar music, and the warm, friendly voice of Eamonn Andrews. The results would follow immediately, sending us into delight or dismay. Brief reports on the top matches came next – the programme has not changed very much in format to the present day, only the reporters. Arthur Appleton would tell us, with his distinctly Geordie accent, about Newcastle or Sunderland. Don Davies would report, with a touch of humour, the goings on at Old Trafford, or Maine Road... or Deepdale. It was all part of Saturday's pattern of events.

After the sausage, egg and chips there was the wait for the Football Post to arrive. That was always a good moment, especially if the result had gone in Preston's favour. 'NORTH END LEAVE IT LATE' would be the headline, or, if they'd been beaten 'PRESTON LOSE BY THE ODD GOAL IN FIVE". Then would follow Walter Pilkington's blow-by-blow account of the afternoon's proceedings. It was all very matter-of-fact. 'Mitchell beat Cunningham on the outside before centering. Robledo (G) allowed the ball to run to Milburn who beat Gooch with a low shot only for Walton to clear off the line... '

And so on... The first half was described at some length, but because of time constraints the later stages were done more sketchily.

'Morrison equalised for Preston in the 87th minute.' Phew! But the reader had to imagine how he'd done it... was it a blistering 20-yarder which nearly ripped the net away from the stanchion, or a scrambled toe-ender from two yards out? If you weren't there you'd never know.

There were no TV cameras to show endless action replays. The Post carried two or three photographs of the early play, and maybe a picture of the first goal. The cameramen were a familiar sighting as they sat beside the goal where they expected the action to be. Getting those

The cameramen...
a familiar sighting

photographs developed and turned into half-tones in time to be included in the football edition was a precise, clockwork procedure, I guess, with little time to spare. As well as Preston, you could read similar accounts of Blackburn's game, and those involving Blackpool, Southport, Chorley, Preston Grasshoppers, Vale of Lune and others. Walter's more considered analysis of Preston's match appeared in the Monday evening edition.

Easter could be a critical period in those days, with three games in four days that could decide a team's destiny. So it was for Preston North End in 1955. On Good Friday a humiliating home defeat by fellow-strugglers Leicester City increased the fears and frustrations of the fans. Arthur Rowley headed a goal past George Thompson from about 25 yards. I can't remember seeing a goal scored from so far out with a header – and this with an old, heavy leather football. Rowley was a prolific goalscorer for over a decade, but for Preston fans this was one time NOT to sit back and admire opposition players. The team were perilously close to the bottom of the table. Finney was clearly not fully fit, but played anyway. The following day another home game, against Bolton, began well with two goals in the first ten minutes, and the nervous spectators relaxed a bit. But in the end Preston were lucky to escape with a draw. Finney limped away at the end, and it was painfully obvious that if North End were to avoid relegation, it would have to be done without their main man.

"At number seven will be Campbell and not Finney… "

Les Campbell was even smaller than Harry Anders, but the goal he scored in the return game at Leicester on Easter Monday was priceless.

Campbell…
a priceless goal

Fred Else replaced Thompson in goal. It was Else's third game only for the first team, but he kept a clean sheet, and Preston won 1-0. In the end, Leicester went down and North End didn't. But with Tom hurt and Marston gone back home, the season ended on a low note. Even an unlikely hat-trick by Ken Waterhouse at Charlton scarcely lifted the gloom.

CHAPTER 10

Harmer the Charmer

During the summer Preston went out and bought Tommy Thompson from Aston Villa for £27,000. Now that lifted our spirits. Thompson had always done well against North End, and there were high hopes that he would do the business for us. Like thousands of Preston fans I was in the crowd at Goodison Park when Thompson made his debut for his new club in August 1955, and can still remember THAT goal.

"He isn't going to shoot from THERE... is he?"

Like most other onlookers I asked myself that question, but more quickly than it takes to tell, the ball was in the Everton net. Tommy Thompson had taken precisely one minute to introduce himself. Finney, apparently fit once more, revelled in the new partnership, and scored twice.

It was 4-0 at half-time. Preston won that, and with Thompson scoring in both, won their next two games as well. It was all so promising, but the bubble soon burst. By the time North End visited Blackpool in October

Tommy Thompson... took precisely one minute to introduce himself...

their form had dipped worryingly. That was the day when, early in the match, George Farm was injured and young Jimmy Armfield pulled on the goalkeeping jersey. Preston scored six and won easily, with every forward getting on the scoresheet. It wouldn't happen today, of course, but they were the days long before substitutes were allowed. Farm came back as an outfield player and headed a consolation goal for Blackpool to raise the biggest cheer of the afternoon.

Tommy Thompson was a success and Finney had a good season, missing fewer games than usual and scoring 17 times. There was no noticeable drop in his powers. Nevertheless Preston hovered just above the relegation zone. A humiliating Cup defeat at West Ham was followed by five successive league reverses, and fans fell into despair.

A good Easter rescued them, Thompson and Finney each scoring twice at White Hart Lane, and a Finney penalty accounted for the Champions Chelsea at the Bridge. The return match with Spurs on Easter Monday was a ding-dong affair with six goals being shared. For the visitors Tommy Harmer gave an exquisite display. You couldn't imagine

Harmer pulled all the strings that day

anyone looking less like a footballer. Athletic, muscular and fast... Harmer was none of these. But he pulled all the strings that day, and for once even Finney had to concede centre stage. The ball was Harmer's except when he allowed others to have it for a while. I hope he took it home with him afterwards. Preston were lucky to escape with a draw, and that single point was all that saved them from the drop. There were TEN home defeats in the League that winter. Is there anything worse than 0-1 at home? North End had FIVE 0-1s in 1955-56, making for a few miserable journies home. Strangely, there were no more 0-1 home reverses for the next four seasons! Frank Hill, who had managed the club for two mediocre seasons, was sacked.

Is there anything worse than 0-1 at home?

The following campaign opened with three losses which did nothing to relieve the gloom. August 1956 was a terrible month. It was during one of those defeats at Chelsea that another famous Finney photograph, The Splash, was taken. Not surprisingly in view of the waterlogged extremities, Tom had ended that match playing down the middle at the request of Jimmy Milne, acting Coach following Frank Hill's departure. Milne then asked Finney to start Preston's next match at CENTRE-FORWARD, with Les Campbell wearing the number seven shirt. News of a fourth straight defeat at Manchester United surprised nobody, but Finney once again did well in the centre. It was a pity that three of those first four defeats were from the only two teams who would finish the season above Preston. Finney's instant success in his new role, along with the appointment of Cliff Britton as Manager, lifted our spirits slightly, but no one was quite ready for the sensational impact about to be made.

Poor Cardiff City, on the receiving end of some large hidings at Deepdale over the years, were the first to feel the Finney blast. Danny Malloy was a fairly decent centre-half who ended up chasing his own shadow. Finney teased and taunted him for 90 minutes, which must have seemed twice as long to Malloy who left the field frothing at the mouth. He also put through his own goal. He did so again in the return match at Ninian Park. I understand Malloy was never the same player again... Preston won 6-0, and their season was under way at last. There followed some terrific performances, and some goals which I can still see in my mind's eye through the mists of time. Sunderland were also hit for six at Deepdale on a day when Les Dagger made such an impressive debut at outside-right, and Tommy Thompson scored a hat-trick. But Finney was again the Master of Ceremonies, scoring twice and assisting in most of the others. The national dailies raved about Finney's displays during those Autumn weeks. One reporter – it may have been Henry Rose of the Express – declared him the 'best number nine since Dean and Lawton'. Certainly he was adding a new dimension to centre-forward play. Although Finney had switched to the middle on a few occasions in previous seasons – mostly in emergencies – it was remarkable to relate that in just a few short weeks he had become the most talked about centre-forward in the land. It was as if he'd never played in any other position. Yet, knowing the man's skill and soccer know-how, his success in the new role was hardly surprising. I really think Finney could have played and succeeded anywhere. Once again the clash with Wolves, at Molyneux, was much anticipated. It brought Finney into direct confrontation with Billy Wright, who had also moved into the middle with ease. Once England's best wing-half, Wright was now England's best centre-half. On the day, Tom gave him the most torrid time, scoring twice and making another for Thompson. Yet incredibly Preston lost to their old adversaries. From 3-0 the score moved to 3-4 in the last 15 minutes as Wolves tore the North End rearguard to ribbons. Harry Hooper, a good but not exceptional winger, chose this day to give his best-ever show and scored a hat-trick. Ray Evans wasn't the only defender to have a nightmare, but he was the one to be summarily replaced. Frank O'Farrell was signed from West Ham, and scored on his debut against Manchester City. Preston won that one, and nearly everything else that season. An accomplished and unflustered wing-half, O'Farrell was the final piece in what was one of the club's best-ever line-ups. He played 17 League games for North End before tasting defeat for the first time. Finney, as everyone predicted, was chosen to play centre-forward for

England firstly against Wales and then Yugoslavia, both at Wembley. The matches were won comfortably enough, and whilst Tom did well it was inconclusive. It always appeared that England would sooner or later revert to the more traditional kind of number nine. Tommy Taylor, a brilliant young striker, seemed a better long-term solution.

I don't think I missed any home matches during this exciting time, and some away grounds were also within reach. As I've written before, the memories fuse into one. I can see, in the mind's eye, the team moving smoothly forward, and scoring, the goalscorer turning to shake hands with his colleagues, all trotting back to the centre for the restart.

Frank O'Farrell... the final piece of the jig-saw, and later to become manager of Manchester United.

Portsmouth got their customary trouncing at Deepdale, this time by 7-1 as Sammy Taylor got his first hat-trick for the club. The little Scot was always on the lookout for goals and had established himself as a firm favourite. On the other wing local lad Les Dagger could be brilliant and infuriating in turn. He never fulfilled the promise of that terrific debut display, but I recall the match at Burnden Park, when he continually tormented the Bolton left-back Threlfall. Finally Dagger was hauled

Dagger was hauled down, shorts around his knees...

down, shorts around his knees, and Finney dispatched the penalty, his second of the afternoon, and Preston won 3-2. So, following their atrocious start to the season, they almost but not quite caught up with the leaders.

All the faithful believed that this side would be the one to bring the FA Cup back to Preston at last. They needed three games to dispose of Sheffield Wednesday in round three, but steamrollered the Yorkshiremen in the second replay at Goodison Park. Thompson scored two of North End's five goals that Monday afternoon. I bunked off school to go. Thompson must have loved playing at Everton. He scored twice in the League game there, making five in three visits since joining Preston. He'd also been a scorer there for Villa in a previous existence. Bristol Rovers were beaten away in the fourth round, Finney scoring twice and missing a penalty-kick. Next North End drew Arsenal at home. It was expected to be the tie of the round and so it proved. With a strong wind at their backs, Arsenal took full advantage from the start. Joe Dunn sliced the ball into his own net early on, to everyone's horror but the Gunners. it was a nightmare first half for the usually secure centre-half, David Herd giving him a desperate chasing. He scored once, I think, but it could have been three or four but for Fred Else. Finney scored from what looked like an offside position, beating

Thompson must have loved playing at Everton...

Sullivan with a thunderbolt, but Arsenal led 3-1 at the interval. Preston came back strongly after the break, as we hoped they would. Attacking the Kop, Finney scored again, and Thompson... but try as they might no winner ensued. Worse, Thompson was injured and missed the replay. The ever-faithful Ken Waterhouse took his place, but it wasn't the same. Beaten at Highbury, Preston bowed out of the Cup for another year.

Cross my heart, I once saw Tom Finney commit a foul. I can't identify the match, or the player offended against, or the referee who shamefacedly had to blow his whistle and point towards the Preston goal. I can't believe it was deliberate. Perhaps Tom was fractionally too late in the tackle, but a foul it was and the ref was right. The crowd was stunned into silence. Did that official leave Deepdale that day in disguise? Did he tell his friends at the Referees' Convention what he'd done? If so, did they believe him? Is the sky big?

CHAPTER 11

Ecstacy and sadness intermingled

In August and September of 1957 Preston surprisingly lost all their first five away matches of the new campaign. They countered this by winning the five games on their own soil, scoring 20 goals and giving their Deepdale following much delight. The average home crowd was only 25,000, which seemed somewhat disappointing considering the great football Finney and company were serving up every time. Portsmouth, as usual, were given a fearful hiding. I spoke with Ray Crawford a few years ago, and he recalled this game. It was one of his first League games – he was 21 at the time – and he particularly remembered Finney's brilliance and Docherty's tackling. Pompey must have hated the prospect of coming to Preston in the 'fifties. So too must Manchester City, who were given their customary thrashing. Trautmann, who had defied North End single-handedly on his first visit in 1952, now looked totally fed up. Since then Preston had put 24

*Trautmann...
totally fed up
by this time.*

goals in City's net in six visits. Chelsea were hammered too, after an
even first half. For Preston fans it was the first opportunity to see the
young phenomenon called Jimmy Greaves. He did little to impress.
How different would be his visit to Deepdale two years hence! But this
time he was upstaged by wee Sammy Taylor, who scored three times
from the left wing. Derek Mayers, bought from Everton, forced his way
into the team in place of Dagger and scored on his debut against Spurs
and regularly thereafter. Following their faltering start, the season
became one of almost unbroken success for Preston and continual
pleasure for their fans. Looking back, it has to be one of my favourite
campaigns as a North End fan, yet was also marked with terrible
sadness. In February 1958 Preston gave one of their most irresistible
performances in beating Birmingham City 8-0. Tom Finney scored a

wonderful goal at the Kop end, swerving past two defenders and beating Gil Merrick with a shot of frightening ferocity. Poor Gil must have felt only the draught. I can still see it now. It was Finney's second, but he couldn't or didn't want to get his hat-trick. Tommy Thompson did get three, as did Taylor, but the old plumber was once again the ringmaster. Birmingham completely surrendered long before the end, and it could have been more than eight. For a few days it was the talk of the town.

But on the Thursday of the following week the plane carrying Manchester United home from Belgrade crashed at Munich, sending football fans everywhere into mourning. Like everyone else, I know exactly where I was when I heard the devastating news. Just a few weeks earlier I had seen these same United players battle out a thrilling 1-1 draw at Preston. Liam Whelan hit an unstoppable volley past Fred

Whelan... an unstoppable volley.

Taylor and Byrne, both gone...

Else at the Kop end. At the same end the amazing Duncan Edwards burst through to beat Else with a scorching shot, only to have the goal mysteriously disallowed. In the same match we had watched Roger Byrne, Tommy Taylor and David Pegg. And now they were gone, all of them. I was 17, and wept openly, unashamedly. Football went on, but it was not quite the same. Preston North End, like most other teams, didn't wish to play the following weekend, but were told they had to, and won a rather hollow victory at Chelsea. When he cracked in a beauty against Sunderland, Thompson had scored in ELEVEN successive League games. Preston's long unbeaten run ended abruptly at Everton with a 4-2 loss. It was one of the few away games I was able to attend that season, and for once North End were second best. Eddie Thomas, a second-rate inside-forward who also had a spell at Ewood, scored all four goals.

Thompson got 34 and Finney 26 out of the club's 100 League goals. From the wings, Mayers and Taylor each got double figures. The Preston Plumber was now 36, and still seemed as potent as ever from centre-forward. Against Leeds United at Deepdale he gave one of his best-ever displays, scoring twice and making the other. It seems strange that Finney NEVER got a hat-trick for the club. Wayman did it seven times, Thompson on three occasions, and even Taylor has three Preston hat-tricks on his CV. Apart from the occasional change, the team remained the same throughout, with fortunately few injuries. They were neck and neck with Wolves for the Championship, but vitally lost both home and away to their rivals. Had they won one and drawn the other then they, not Wolves, would have been Champions.

I think it was at the end of that season when Arsenal, too, were given a bit of a hiding at Deepdale. A tall, ungainly centre-half called Jim Fotheringham, with a terrible haircut, had a nightmare experience against Finney who ran past him first on one side and then the other and then through his long legs... I understand slim Jim never played again for Arsenal after that.

Disappointingly, Preston went out of the FA Cup without putting up much of a fight. Bolton beat them much too easily at Deepdale, by 3-0. It was decided to play Dennis Hatsell at centre-forward and Finney on the left. Looking back, it was a sad selection. Both Finney and Hatsell were fairly ineffective, and Bolton were much the better team on the day. Ray Parry scored twice for Bolton. One of them, at the Kop end,

was with a shot so hard that it burst through Else's hands. Preston reverted to their usual line-up the following Saturday and beat West Brom comfortably. If only...

Finney didn't play in either match with Wolves. The second one clashed with the England v Scotland encounter at Hampden. You may remember, as I do, how Tom skipped around Alex Parker to set up a first International goal for Bobby Charlton. But Preston fans would have preferred their man to have been doing it at Molyneux. Finney went as a winger with England to the World Cup in Sweden but played in only one match. His penalty-kick, placed accurately out of the reach of Lev Yashin, saved the first match with Russia. Tom was kicked up and down and out of the tournament. Robbed of three great players by the Munich air crash, England could have gambled and played Bobby Charlton and even taken the young Jimmy Greaves, but stayed with the old guard and went out with barely a whimper.

CHAPTER 12

Any old Tom, Dick or Harry

One of the chief differences between the 'fifties and the noughties was the appreciation which was given in those days to visiting players. Every opposing team had at least one star of some magnitude, and we could look forward with a kind of anticipation to their coming. As a boy Neville Cardus used to pray thus:

"Please God, let Victor Trumper score a century today for Australia against England – out of 137 all out."

My supplication was along the same lines:

"Lord, let Jackie Milburn score two spectacular goals at Deepdale tomorrow, but let Preston win 3-2 anyway."

I liked Milburn. He was my kind of whole-hearted footballer. I wished like mad he would be transferred to Preston, but like so many in those days Milburn was a one-club man. Wor Jackie could win a match on his own, when the rest of his team were listless and impotent, as he did in the FA Cup Final against Blackpool. In a match in 1955 Preston were comfortable at 3-0 until Milburn stirred himself. Two wonderful goals had North End wobbling and hanging on at the final whistle to win 4-3. Other visiting performers frequently decorate my mental sketchbook. Most teams had a midfield player who made them tick. I've talked

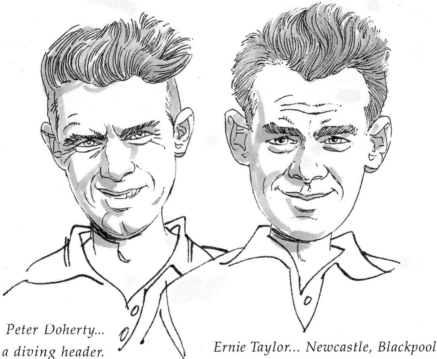

Peter Doherty...
a diving header.

Ernie Taylor... Newcastle, Blackpool
and Manchester United

elsewhere about Tommy Harmer and Len Shackleton and Raich Carter. I can remember, too, Jimmy Hagan of Sheffield United and Arsenal's Jimmy Logie both having fine games at Deepdale. Some of them didn't run around a lot, much less tackle back. The defensive side of their game, or lack of it, would be unacceptable today. But with exquisite passes, men like these would prompt and scheme and direct the play,

*Eddie Baily
of Spurs and
England*

and were ever pleasing to the eye. Middlesbrough's Wilf Mannion I saw, too, in his later years – truly he was the golden boy of English soccer. Ernie Taylor of Newcastle and later with Blackpool was one of the smallest players on view, yet could win a game with one decisive move. Portsmouth's Len Phillips played only a handful of games for England, yet I recall him one afternoon at Preston giving a perfect example of inside-forward play. Although I can't identify the match, or the result of the match, his twinkling feet nevertheless are imprinted on my memory. I met an ageing Len Phillips many years later in Portsmouth, and he spoke to me affectionately of Finney both as an opponent and as a colleague for England. "Tom was the best I ever saw," he said.

I liked Peter Doherty. I remember Uncle Will rhapsodysing about the goal he scored at Goodison Park against England, to snatch a draw for Northern Ireland from the jaws of defeat. "He just threw himself at it… out of nowhere! Diving header, tha knows? Swift no chance… "

Horatio Carter…
a genius, but
extremely
naughty one day
at Preston.

Doherty, too, was on his last legs when he came to Preston in 1951 in a Doncaster side which was overwhelmingly outclassed. Doherty was still able to rise above the mediocrity of his colleagues and give a display of passing and dribbling of international quality.

Duncan Edwards - the finest young player of all time? Had he survived, there would have been no room for Bobby Moore...

In his all-too-short career Duncan Edwards appeared several times at Preston. There was a noticeable intake of breath when he first ran out on to the Deepdale pitch in February 1954. Though only 17, this youth was built like an Adonis, and had thighs with the circumference of tree trunks. It was clear that day that we were watching someone very special. When those young legs began pumping there appeared nothing could stand in his way. By the time of his untimely death in 1958 Edwards was the ideal specimen of manhood, the perfect footballer. He was the finest young player that I, for one, ever saw. In what was to be his last appearance at Preston, in November 1957, he gave the perfect demonstration of midfield play. He could tackle, pass, run with the ball and shoot with exceptional power. In short, Edwards had everything. Had he survived, there would have been no room for Bobby Moore in the England team. Not at left-halfback, anyway. There was the same

John Charles - the Gentle Giant.

kind of gasp when John Charles took the field at Preston in 1957. I'm sure that Charles must have played here some years before, in the Second Division, as a young centre-half, but later Leeds United converted him to striker and his 40 goals in one season helped them back into the top flight. He was an awesome figure, and in his only season in Division One he scored 38 times. He had few chances to add to that number at Deepdale because Leeds spent most of the afternoon on the defensive, and lost decisively. But Charles left a clear impression, an extraordinary, larger than life footballer. At the end of the season he went to ply his trade in Italy, where they dubbed him "Il Gigante Buono"- the Gentle Giant.

Joe Mercer...
wonderfully
successful for
Everton, Arsenal
and England.

There were other half-backs who also left a mark on the memory. Some have been talked about elsewhere in this essay, but I also recall Jimmy

Dickinson with affection. Finney and Dickinson always exchanged warm handshakes before and after the match, although Portsmouth hardly ever enjoyed any success at Deepdale during the 'fifties. Even so the wing-half could be depended upon for an immaculate display every time. Along with Billy Wright he was one of England's better half-backs in the period leading up to the World Cup in Sweden in 1954. It wasn't a happy tournament for Jimmy and he scored a disastrous own-goal against Belgium. But like Finney he was a one-club-man throughout his long illustrious career, and earned the respect of fans up and down the land. So did Blackpool's Harry Johnston. He deserved his FA Cup winners' medal gained at the third attempt in 1953, but the same year he experienced the opposite humiliating emotions at the feet of the magical Magyars at Wembley.

*Happy Harry
after the 1953
FA Cup Final...*

CHAPTER 13

Into the net, with or without the ball...

Goalkeeping was different in the 'fifties. Not better than it is today, but not always worse. Just different, like the game itself. For one thing, goalies got less protection from referees. Goalies were bundled or shoulder-charged into the net with the ball, quite fairly, and the goal was awarded. Goalies were often bundled into the net without the ball, just for fun, and to warn them that there was a big foe on the prowl. In tricky situations goalkeepers needed to have enough foresight to punch and not to catch. Some, like Frank Swift, could punch vast distances.

I didn't see Swifty in the flesh. His best days were before the war, although he did keep the England jersey for a few years after, and reserved one of his greatest displays until the last, in Turin, 1948. The big man captained his country that day and rose to the occasion with a brilliant, defiant exhibition. At home he played for Manchester City, winning FA Cup and Championship medals in the 'thirties. He became

a journalist and sadly was one of those killed at Munich in 1958. The first time I saw City at Preston Bert Trautmann had become their custodian, and I've spoken of him elsewhere. There never was a braver man than Bert, and when he broke his neck in the 1956 FA Cup Final it was purely as a result of his courage. Unlike today, 'keepers could fall upon or pick up back passes without fear of infringement. They would then bounce the ball several times on the move before booting it clear,

always out of their hands. Not as we see today, the slow dribble out of the area and the long kick off the ground. Because the ball was heavier, a kick beyond the halfway line was quite an achievement for a goalie. The only variation was the throw, which some goalies specialised in, and there were those who could throw a long way.

Fred Else... the best goalie never to play for England.

I saw Ken Grieves in goal for Bolton once, and he was a good thrower. Soccer was his winter job, the Australian being better known for his run-scoring and slip-catching for Lancashire in the summer months. Those who were present, as I was, will remember his magnificent century the first time County Cricket came to Southport in 1958.

Aussie Ken Grieves... goalkeeping was his winter job.

Footballer-cricketers were always a curiosity, not uncommon in the 'fifties but non-existent today. I never saw Denis Compton on the football field but was fortunate enough to watch him get a wonderful hundred against South Africa at Old Trafford. His brother Leslie played a few times for Arsenal at Deepdale, as did Arthur Milton, Willie Watson (Sunderland), Ken Taylor (Huddersfield), Henry Horton (Blackburn) and Derek Ufton and Stuart Leary of Charlton. For Charlton, Sam Bartram was a goalie par excellence. Single-handedly he held a hungry attack at bay on that emotional evening when North End played their first home match back in Division One in 1951. But like King Canute, even Sam could not keep back the tide and in the end he was beaten by a Willie Forbes thunderbolt, then twice more.

After Swift took off his gloves Bert Williams and Ted Ditchburn vied for the yellow England jersey. Both were fit and agile 'keepers and just when you thought the ball had gone past them, out came the spectacular dive and the fingertip save. Preston fans had the opportunity to see and compare them in those exciting FA Cup ties in early 1952. Finney-inspired, North End's attack was too persistent for Williams and before the end he sat down in the Deepdale mud and held up a gloved hand in mock surrender. Ditchburn didn't give in, however, and in the face of a gale-force wind and wave after wave of attacks, performed heroics. Preston fans cursed steady Ted that day. But he'd earned their undying respect. Jack Kelsey of Wales and Arsenal was also one of the very best goalkeepers of the decade. Arsenal always took pride in their defensive organisation, and Kelsey fitted smoothly into that machine. Preston's forwards had many encounters with acrobatic Jack, sometimes winning the battle and sometimes not. There

Acrobatic
Jack Kelsey...

was one special evening in September 1956 when Finney, just converted to centre-forward, fought a lone battle with Kelsey. The Welshman was as defiant as usual until Tom's plunging header left him bewitched, bothered and bewildered all at the same time. In my mind's eye I can see Ron Simpson of Newcastle and United's Harry Gregg making gymnastic saves at the Town End, although I can't identify the matches. Not every goalie had the agility of those mentioned above. Some were heavy and cumbersome, and went down slowly like a sack of potatoes. I remember one, who shall be nameless, flopping down so late he was almost posthumous.

Jimmy Gooch... a great shame when a bad injury hastened the end of his career.

The first Preston goalkeeper I remember was Jimmy Gooch, well loved by the fans on the Kop who always gave him a special reception when he threw his cap and gloves into the net. He was wonderfully dependable, safe as a locked door, and it was a great shame when a bad injury hastened the end of his career. Malcolm Newlands played when Gooch couldn't, but he was more fallible and when Manchester United

stuck five past him in the first half, Preston were quick to sign a replacement. George Thompson was the man. He was good, but not great, and the errors still occured. He had a couple of bad days, and Preston lost the Championship for want of a single point. If only...

The errors still occured...

Thompson, a cartoonist in his spare time, gave steady service for four seasons but he too was history as soon as young Fred Else was ready to take his place between the sticks. About Fred, I've written elsewhere.

Goalkeepers, the barmy lot… did I see one of them once throw his cap at the ball as it flew past him? It may have been Ugolini or Uprichard. Or it may have been the Hesketh Bank goalie, against Fleetwood Hesketh. Or is my memory playing those tricks on me once more?

Did he throw his cap
at the ball?

CHAPTER 14

"You should have seen Fred Else... "

One of the Lancashire venues I'd never yet been to was Old Trafford. The cricket ground, yes, but football no. So on a mild October evening in 1958 some friends and I piled into a van and drove to Manchester to see United play Preston. Manchester United had not yet recovered from the effects of the Munich crash, and were a strange mixture of youth and experience. Bobby Charlton was there, and Alex Dawson, both later to become Deepdale favourites. By this time North End were an ageing team, and it was beginning to show. Docherty had gone (to Arsenal) and Walton, Cunningham, Dunn, O'Farrell, Thompson and Baxter had all left their best years behind them. Finney was still shining brightly, although he was not the player of the early and mid 'fifties either. This was barely discernable, but nevertheless true. He was 36, and still in the England team. We all hoped he would go on playing into his forties, like Matthews, but his body had taken more punishment than the Blackpool man's. That night at Old Trafford Tom was back at outside-left, with Mayers on the right wing and Hatsell centre-forward. Hatsell scored a stonking goal in the first half. Harry Gregg could barely blink as the ball flew past him, and Thompson got an equally good one late in the game. I think they were Preston's only attacks of a one-sided match. The rest was one-way traffic – towards Fred Else's goal. And Fred, bless him, saved everything Charlton, Dawson and company threw at him. In my mind's eye I swear I can see three United attackers bearing down on the Preston goal, and not a defender in sight. But still

Not a defender in sight...

Else defiantly kept his goal intact. North End won 2-0, a travesty of a result. It was one of the two finest goalkeeping displays I ever witnessed, live – equal to that of Trautmann at Deepdale in 1952. Whenever people talk about inspired performances in goal, such as Tomaszewsky against England, I say, "Yes, but you should have seen Fred Else at Old Trafford." Else was unquestionably the best goalie never to win an International cap.

A few days later Finney played for England for the 76th and last time. Preston fell away after the win at United. There were some good displays mixed with some mediocre ones. Hatsell was doing a good job at number nine, but there were those who felt Finney would do a better one. I recall the match against Newcastle which added fuel to this argument. Len White had a great game for the visitors, and North End trailed 1-3 and were seemingly out of it until Finney switched to the centre and scored two excellent goals at the Kop end, one with a header. Newcastle spoiled the story by breaking away to get the winning goal. The centre-forward dispute was not resolved, as from this point on Finney was once again dogged by injury and played only the occasional game. Else also missed some important games, but 16 year-old John Barton made a wonderful debut in goal at Highbury, helping Preston to a 2-1 win. He then let in a rather soft goal at Blackpool on Christmas Day, and went from hero to zero in the space of a few days. Worse, Finney limped off and didn't play again until the last match of the season. The FA Cup briefly revived the spirits of Preston's followers. Even without their main man, North End made steady progress to the Fifth Round. Young Alex Farrall scored some good goals as Second Division Derby County were eliminated. I can still see another young player, wing-half Jim Smith, striding through to shoot a thrilling goal at

Jim Smith in full stride...

the Kop end as Preston won the replay 4-2. Bradford City, another lower League side, put up a great fight and only a late shot by O'Farrell at the Town end saw North End through that one. After knocking out Preston the previous year Bolton had gone on to win the Cup. Now these famous old Lancashire rivals were once again paired with each other in round five, this time at Burnden Park. It was a brave performance on the day, and Preston should have won. As it was they needed Tommy Thompson's late penalty to get themselves a draw. Thompson scored from the rebound after Eddie Hopkinson saved his first shot. Over 37,000 saw the replay. It could not have been all-ticket, because some of my friends were locked out when the gates were closed. Once again Preston were on the point of going out of the Cup, but Smith raced upfield to head a last-gasp equaliser and send the tie into extra-time, and from there to a second replay, this time at Ewood Park. No penalty shoot-outs in those days! Nat Lofthouse eventually settled the tie at the third attempt, although Hatsell missed a gilt-edged opportunity for Preston. The combined attendances at the three matches added up to 147,000. Many people, like myself, must have seen all three... There wasn't much to cheer after that as North End finished mid-table. Jimmy Baxter played his 245th and last League match for the club before going back to Barnsley. He marked it with a goal.

Home matches were lost, and attendances at Deepdale plummeted. Only 10,000 watched a goalless horror show with Luton. Villa came needing a win to escape the relegation dogfight. They'd NEVER lost at Preston throughout the whole decade. But even without Finney, Villa were well beaten this time. Tommy Thompson scored twice against his old mates. It was the height of irony. Villa went down, when one point would have saved them. They had been Preston's bogey team more than any other. Even Manchester United were beaten occasionally, and Wolves and West Brom. But we all knew that when Villa came to town there was nothing in it for North End.Finney came back to play in the last game of the season, a 2-2 draw with Spurs. Davie Sneddon, signed from Dundee, made his debut in that match, replacing Baxter. A mighty impressive debut it was, too, as he made a goal for Thompson with a

After knocking out Preston, Bolton went on to win the Cup in 1958...

glorious defence-splitting pass. Finney looked stiff, but we comforted ourselves with the thought that the old boy would be fit and ready for the new campaign in August.

CHAPTER 15

End of an era

Sure enough, when the new season began in August 1959, Tom Finney was there in a familiar Preston line-up, apparently fit and ready to go. The only fairly new face was Sneddon. Tom scored once as North End came back from a seemingly hopeless position (1-4 down with ten minutes to go) to draw 4-4 at Stamford Bridge. I, along with all the other fans, thought all was well. But Finney was already considering retirement, and some time during that Autumn, Winter or Spring he decided he'd had enough. The body and the legs couldn't take any more. So, in March, after another gallant attempt to win the FA Cup had failed, it was made public. "TOM FINNEY TO RETIRE" announced the morning papers. Even to those who saw it coming, it was shockingly final.

The early weeks of Tom Finney's last season had promised good things. In October and November North End won nine games out of ten, and in December, when Chelsea visited Deepdale, they were TOP of Division One – an exalted position they were never to reach again. Top of Division One, yes, in 2006 – but we all know that by then Division One was in fact Division Two... Manchester United were given a rare but emphatic beating, 4-0, and the following week Blackburn were on the wrong end of a 4-1 scoreline at Ewood – displays which were as good as any I could remember. Arsenal were beaten 3-0 at Highbury, when Joe Walton scored one of the goals. Not a prolific scorer, jolly Joe managed just four in 401 League games. There was a 4-3 win over Wolves, a real ding-dong affair like so many matches against the men in old gold. There were lots of good goals in this one, the best being one

Alston chipped the ball over Finlayson...

by Alex Alston at the Kop end, when he chipped the ball over Finlayson from a long way out. Chelsea, and Jimmy Greaves in particular, emphatically ended Preston's unbeaten run. Coming home from that match, I think most of the fans knew that the League Championship

PRESTON 4 CHELSEA 5

IT WAS A GLOOMY DAY AT DEEPDALE, IN EVERY SENSE. THE SLOWNESS OF THE HOME DEFENCE WAS FULLY SHOWN. THERE WAS A HOLE SO WIDE YOU COULD HAVE DRIVEN A SLEDGE AND REINDEER THROUGH.

PRESTON WERE LEADING 2-1 AFTER 20 MINUTES, AND THE FANS WERE HAPPY—AS FAR AS WE COULD TELL...

IF THE SCORE STAYS LIKE THIS WE SHOULD WIN.

SADLY, THE SCORE DIDN'T STAY LIKE THAT. THE LONGER THE GAME WENT ON, NORTH END'S PLACE AT THE TOP OF THE FIRST DIVISION LOOKED MORE VAIN AND INSECURE.

MMM..., KISS KISS...

LADY GODIVA HAD MORE COVER THAN POOR FRED ELSE,

YOUNG JIMMY GREAVES MUST HAVE THOUGHT ALL OF HIS BIRTHDAYS HAD COME AT ONCE, SO MUCH TIME AND SPACE WAS HE ALLOWED,

SOMEBODY FASTEN HIS BOOTLACES TOGETHER...

TOMMY THOMPSON SCORED THREE HIMSELF, JUST TO KEEP THE GAME CLOSE.

BUT GREAVES UPSTAGED EVERYONE, FINNEY INCLUDED, HE LOOKS A SURE-FIRE BET TO WIN ENGLAND THE WORLD CUP ONE DAY,...

was not a realistic target. Greaves scored FIVE times, underlining how fragile North End's defence could be. The home side certainly made a game of it nevertheless, losing only by 4-5. Thompson couldn't quite do a Greaves, but collected a hat-trick.

It was one of a succession of eleven Division One games without a win, a sad sequence which saw them fall from the top of the league to halfway down.

Finney made one last valiant attempt to win the FA Cup for Preston and for himself. I was able to see all six matches, including replays, and Tom played at centre-forward in all of these exciting encounters. It wasn't easy progress. The ageing team were a bit fortunate to escape with a draw at Stoke's old Victoria Ground in Round Three before winning the replay in front of a 35,000 crowd. Finney scored one of the goals in a 3-1 win. There was a terrific scrap at Bristol Rovers, the second visit to Eastville in four years. After a 3-3 draw the teams returned to Preston the following Tuesday and again shared six goals but this time Bristol only got one of them.

Brighton gave North End a fright but were narrowly eliminated, setting up a much anticipated clash with Aston Villa in Round Six. Nearly 70,000 crowded into Villa Park and saw the home side end Preston's challenge 2-0, Gerry Hitchens scoring the all-important opener with a

Hitchens' shot took a wicked deflection...

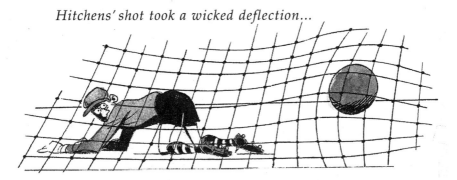

wickedly deflected shot. Else went one way, the ball went the other, and with it went North End's hopes and dreams. It was a sad Preston following who returned north that evening by car and coach and train… I suspect most of us knew that marked the end of the road for Tom. He would never win that medal. He played on, and in an excellent 4-1 win over Blackpool he scored what turned out to be his last goal for the old club.

North End's youth team provided an exciting diversion at this time, reaching the Final of the FA Youth Cup before going down to Chelsea, and Bobby Tambling in particular. George Ross, Tug Wilson, Peter Thompson and Alan Spavin gave hope for the future.

Enough has been documented about Tom Finney's last match against Luton Town. It was a game no one wanted to come, yet everyone was compelled to attend just to say 'Thank you and farewell' to the man who had graced this field for all those years. The game, which Preston won, seemed irrelevant and afterwards Tom spoke eloquently to the crowd who stayed simply because they had nowhere else to go and didn't want to let their hero go.

The match seemed irrelevant...

Crisp Smith bags a cracker...

Farewell to a genius...

It was the end of an era, and a convenient place to end these nostalgic scribblings. Thank you to all the players and fans who made those years so enjoyable.